A Forager's Guide to Appreciating Nature

Foraging Tips for Beginners and Experts Alike

T. J. Crow

ISBN: 979-8-5924-3798-4

DEDICATION

I would like to dedicate this book to all foragers, regardless of experience level, and to those who wish to learn more about this fun pastime. The world is full of beauty and wonder. It is no small accomplishment to realize this and to take steps to learn more.

CONTENTS

ACKNOWLEDGMENTS

There are so many people who have helped me in my journey toward becoming a writer. In fact, there are too many to name here, which is an unfortunate fact that I must face. To friends and family who do not see their name, please know that I still greatly value your feedback and guidance.

I would first like to thank Mom and Dad for supporting this little hobby for all these years. Thank you for encouraging me to pursue this goal and for never letting me give up.

I would like to thank my husband for his continuous support and willingness to be one of the first people I show a piece of work to. Thank you for your honest feedback and advice. You've helped me grow significantly as a writer.

Thank you to my father-in-law and mother-in-law for your support and for guiding me on the road to getting this little book published.

Thank you to Dr. Tess of Liberty University. You inspired me to inspire others.

Thank you to all my friends who have to put up with me randomly messaging them at the wee hours of the morning (when any normal person would be deep asleep) with a declaration of a new idea—in all caps lock. I really don't know how you all put up with me! Thank you for your support and patience.

And thank you to Sarah, who inspired me to write all those years ago.

INTRODUCTION

When you look at a vast expanse of trees, what do you see? Do you see a place for a thriving city with sky-high towers and elaborate structures? Perhaps you might see a location for a small subdivision with a close-knit community. You might even see a state park where people can gather and kids can play and nature envelops its visitors. Regardless of what you see, there is one truth that stands out: a forest provides opportunities for dreaming – even if some dreams drastically change the forest itself.

When I see a forest, I see adventure. I see a land that I have explored a hundred times over, yet still don't fully know. I see a land with hidden secrets and bountiful harvests. I see beauty. I see hardship. I see growth, perseverance, and strength. I see what humanity strives to be, in a way.

I didn't always see the forest this way. It was something that was simply "there," and I often took it for granted. My change in perspective happened slowly over time and was mostly self-taught. The more I learned about the world around us, the more inspired I became. The more inspired I became, the more I wanted to show people what I saw. Thus, I created this guide in the hopes that someday it might help somebody else who has taken their first steps on the path toward appreciating nature.

This guide combines both advice and descriptions of my own experiences. After multiple drafts and outlines, I found this to be the most effective way for the guide to be written. This style of guide will certainly not be for everybody and some may find it off-putting; however, it is my hope, Dear Reader, that you find it enjoyable enough in your own way.

Now then, enough with the introductory statements. Let's move on to the guide, shall we?

Ghost Plant (*Monotropa uniflora*). Photo credit T. J. Crow

STEP ONE: GATHER YOUR GEAR

It is important to have the proper gear while walking through the forest, particularly if one plans on becoming a forager (a person who hunts for wild food sources) or a mushroom hunter. The woodlands can hold many surprises, from hidden roots to camouflaged snakes to steep hills. If you don't have the right gear, you could end up injured or lost. This isn't meant to scare you away from exploring or foraging; it is simply meant to cement the importance of being prepared and protecting yourself.

The gear that I use is based off of a guide by The Modern Forager, which provides an excellent list that can apply to people of all experience levels. Items on the Modern Forager's list include the following:

- Hiking boots or shoes
- Rain gear
- A canteen or water bottle
- Map and compass or GPS device
- Knife
- Backpack
- Basket or mesh bag if foraging
- Snacks
- A noise maker or whistle

I personally don't use everything on this list (I hardly ever bring any rain gear, admittedly), and I do bring a few additional items that are not on the list. These extra items include a snake bite kit, a first aid kit, a sturdy stick for finding hidden mushrooms and scaling steeper hills, and (whenever I can remember it) bug spray for my legs. The area in which I live becomes bursting at the seams with seed ticks during a certain time of year, and their preferred delicacy seems to be leg blood. Having hundreds of itchy little bites on one's legs is not a pleasant feeling, but the bug spray deters most of them. As additional leg protection, I also wear a pair of jeans or other long pants. I have also found that having thick socks protects one's heels.

Once you have your gear, you're ready for the next step.

Devil's Urn (*Urnula craterium*). Photo credit T. J. Crow.

STEP TWO: OBSERVE FROM THE OUTSIDE

Now that you have your gear, you're ready to start on your adventure! By this point, you're likely ready to get going and want to rush into the woods. Here's a small piece of advice: don't.

People are always rushing about in their day to day lives. We have to hurry and finish errands. We have to hurry and get to work. We have to hurry and go grocery shopping. We have to hurry and go to bed. We have to hurry and wake up so we can hurry all over again.

Don't be in a rush to enter the forest. It's not going anywhere; at least, not today, it isn't. Today, you can relax. Stand in front of the forest and just look at it from the outside. You'll be in it soon enough. Do you see that path just to the right, a path that is so worn out from thousands of pairs of feet that its loose dust can be stirred by even the softest whisper of a breeze? Do you see those two tall, old, moss-covered trees standing sentry beside it, protecting it and its travelers? Do you see the line of younger trees and undergrowth forming a border between the tame world you are used to and the wild, fantastical world of the forest? Do you see the grand beauty you are about to enter? Do you feel that rush of excitement flowing wildly through your veins?

It is important to take the time to see the forest from the outside because you can see all this and more. You can also see any berries, flowers, or mushrooms that are within easy reach on the border. Taking a moment to stand and observe the forest gives you time to breathe in fresh air and get into the right mindset for adventuring. You are bracing yourself for all the secrets and wonders the forest holds. How many of those secrets will you uncover today? How many things will surprise you? What are you expecting to see? What do you hope to see?

Once you have asked yourself these questions and feel content with your observation, you are ready to go in and be among the trees—and to take the next step.

Bird's Nest Fungus (*Nidulariaceae* family). Photo credit T. J. Crow.

STEP THREE: OBSERVE FROM THE INSIDE

Congratulations! You've now entered the wild kingdom of the trees, the fantastical court of the insects, and the mysterious realm of things that grow without our notice. So, what do you do now?

Simple. You observe once again!

I heard that exasperated sigh, Dear Reader. I know how you feel. But this is a different kind of observation. This is where the exploration truly begins! Before you go on your way, you have to get a feel for the inside of the woods. What do you see? Trees, of course. Tall trees, small trees, pine trees, oak trees, dead trees—so many trees! There's also a lot of undergrowth. That bush over there looks pleasant and is covered with yellow flowers. Meanwhile, the bush on the other side of the path looks a little more tangled and unpleasant. These things that you are seeing are obvious things.

Take a closer look. The bigger things, like the trees, are easy to see, but there's just something about that tangled bush. It's caught your interest. That's a good sign. That means you can take your first step forward, because now you're invested in your adventure. At this point, you can walk to the bush and might find out that it's full of ripe, juicy blackberries that are ready to pick and place in your basket so you can enjoy them with a bowl of sugar later (only after you've properly identified them, of course).

This is only an example of what can happen if you take the time to observe the woods around you. It is important to get a lay of the land, observe the terrain, and really look at things. You might even notice something small, like a snail making its way across the path. Look for things that catch your attention, and then take a deeper look at those things. Feel free to take pictures, even if you're going to be the only person admiring the pictures later on. This is your adventure, so document it in any way that you like!

Wood Ear (*Auricularia auricula-judae*). Photo credit T. J. Crow

5. STEP FOUR: IDENTIFYING THINGS

Now that you've gone into the woods and have started wandering around, you're likely finding many things that are unfamiliar. In the beginning, you might walk by them without a second thought; however, humans are an inherently curious species and eventually you'll want to know about the things you encounter. Luckily, thanks to the digital age we are in, there are plenty of resources that are literally in your hand at any given moment (if you have a smartphone, that is).

Say, for example, you come across a particularly eye-catching plant. Its clumps of bright white flowers practically glow in the sunlight and its long, jagged leaves look both beautiful and menacing. For a moment, you find yourself imagining that the groups of flowers are gaggles of tiny faeries gossiping about the ever busy squirrels and bees while the dark dagger-like leaves below them protect them from any dangers that might approach. Deep in the back of your mind – or, perhaps, in a more prominent position in your thoughts – you wonder what this plant is.

The first step that many foragers take in exploring something that is new to them is using an identification app on their phone. I'm particular toward the Seek app by iNaturalist. Though it does have some trouble with a few specimens, I've found it to be the most reliable app I've used. It provides a good starting point as you delve into research, which will be covered next.

It might also help to join some Facebook groups. There is an identification group for everything you could possibly encounter on your adventure! Here is what you'll need:

- Clear photos
- Photos from multiple angles
- The color
- The smell
- Location (region) it was found
- Growing conditions
- Growing pattern (single, in groups, clump, etc.

Some of my favorite identification groups are in the Author's Note section in the back.

Catclaw Briar (*Mimosa nutalli*). Photo credit T.J. Crow

6. STEP FIVE: RESEARCHING YOUR FINDS

Now that you've identified whatever caught your attention, it's time to research it! Because this step is so important, I will take more pages than the other steps to guide you. Your life could depend on the research you do, so this step should not be taken lightly. There are several things you should take into consideration while doing research:

The Source: You want to make sure your source is reliable. Is the author of your source an expert, or at least experienced, in the field? Is your source up to date? Does your source have any spelling or grammar mistakes? Is the source backed up by other sources? These are some of the questions you should consider when looking for proper sources.

Some of my favorite sources include the Missouri Department of Conservation's online field guide, which is specific to my state; Mushrooms Demystified by David Arora, because it has a step-by-step guide for identifying mushrooms in any region; the Audubon Society's Field Guide to Mushrooms, which provides more information on mushrooms in North America; the Lady Bird Johnson Center, which provides basic yet pertinent information about various wildflowers across North America; and some local experts I have met while exploring.

Possible Lookalikes: Nature is full of mimicry. It's how things survive. Because some edible plants and mushrooms have toxic lookalikes, it is important to be able to distinguish between what is safe and what isn't. For example, one of my favorite mushrooms, the wood blewit (*Clitocybe nuda/Lepista nuda*) has toxic lookalikes. According to Maxine Stone, past president of the Missouri Mycological Society and author of Missouri's Wild Mushrooms, wood blewits and their lookalikes, some Cortinarius species, grow during the same time of year and in roughly the same areas. However, she also provides information on how to tell them apart, such as a cobwebby veil on the Cortinarius species and the color of the spore print.

Meanwhile, some of the more common toxic plants might have a beneficial lookalike, as is the case between the deadly white snakeroot (*Ageratina altissima*), which was responsible for many deaths in the early days, including Abraham Lincoln's mother, according to Ohio State University, and the medicinal late boneset (*Eupatorium serotinum*), as detailed by the Lady Bird Johnson Wildflower Center. Other plants or mushrooms, such as Chicken of the Woods (*Laetiporus* species) might not have any known toxic lookalikes.

The Specifics: Although it is impossible to remember all the specifics for everything you encounter, it is still important to read through the details of what you find, partly because it helps you to train yourself in looking for certain things. Where is the specimen growing? If it's a mushroom, what's the gill structure? If it's a fruit, how many seeds does it have? Is it growing near any certain trees, or is it on a path or in a clearing? What is the leaf shape? These and other questions can help in your research of whatever you find. Field guides, whether physical or digital, are some of the most reliable sources for determining the specific details of a plant, mushroom, or berry.

Gem-Studded Puffball (*Lycoperdon perlatum*). Photo credit T. J. Crow.

7. STEP SIX: ENJOY WHAT YOU FIND

You now know some information about something you've found. What do you do now? How can you express your appreciation of the piece of nature that you've come across?

To be honest, there's not really a right or wrong answer to this. Everybody expresses their appreciation for nature in different ways. It's really a matter of personal preference. Below are some of the ways that I appreciate nature:

Pictures: I love photography, and I love nature, so it's no small surprise that I have taken up nature photography. One excellent guide that helped me become a better photographer is Josh Dunlop's guide on the Expert Photography website. Reading his guide and others like it will help you get quality pictures of anything you come across.

Studying: When I find a wild thing I like, I become obsessed with it. I can tell you all the differences between wild grapes and their deadly lookalike, moonseed. I can tell somebody, in full detail without having to look up any information, how the amatoxins in most Amanita mushrooms (such as the infamous Death Cap, *Amanita phalloides*) work in the human body. I can even tell you about the male and female parts of some plants and how they must work together if the plant has any hope of producing any fruit that year. Going down rabbit holes of information is just as fun as finding a literal rabbit hole in the wild!

Cooking: I like food. Who doesn't? Food, when cooked properly, is delicious and it's necessary for our survival. When I find something edible in the woods, I like to try it. I always leave at least half of it behind, though; it's only proper to leave some behind for local wildlife. This is one of the unspoken rules among foragers when it comes to respecting the world we are exploring.

One of my favorite edible finds is the Chicken of the Woods mushroom. True to its name, it really is like eating chicken in both flavor and texture! Some recipes for it and other tasty things can be found in guidebooks such as Bo Brown's book Foraging the Ozarks: Finding, Identifying, and Preparing Wild Edible Foods in the Ozarks and even on the Missouri Department of Conservations' website.

I also like to set culinary goals for myself. For example, this upcoming spring and summer, I would like to try some recipes for redbud jelly, violet jelly, and dandelion jelly, which uses the flowers of each of the plants mentioned.

Writing: It is easy to become inspired by what you find in nature. A Chicken of the Woods mushroom, with its fiery orange and yellow colors, can be described as a piece of fallen sunset on the ground. The berries of the fragrant sumac can be likened to small red rubies and the flower of the Catclaw Briar can be described as a bright firework of color. There are so many ways to paint an image in the minds of readers simply by describing the plants, mushrooms, and animals you like. You can use your words to inspire others to start on the path toward appreciating nature, just as I used my words to (hopefully) inspire at least some of the people who read this guide.

So, there you have it! I hope you found this simple guide informative and entertaining enough to start your own adventure. And remember, you don't have to explore the world in the exact same style that I do. Everybody explores in different ways! Just remember to be mindful of federal, state, and local laws if you decide to forage public property. Here in Missouri, it is fine to harvest in public areas as long as one does not try to sell their bounty, according to the Department of Natural Resources. Be sure to check your state's laws before you pick anything,

Never consume anything unless you are 100% certain of the identification and have received confirmation from more experienced foragers. Even if you are 99% certain of the identification, that 1% can be the difference between a good day and a bad day (I've personally experienced this). A good rule of thumb with anything that is harvested is "when in doubt, throw it out!"

Chicken of the Woods (*Laetiporus* species). Photo credit T. J. Crow.

AUTHOR'S NOTE

Throughout the guide, I have mentioned several sources that I extensively use. Sources that you might find helpful are listed below:

Arora, David. Mushrooms Demystified. Ten Speed Press. 1986.

Brown, Bo. Foraging the Ozarks: Finding, Identifying, and Preparing Wild Edible Foods in the Ozarks. Falcon Guides. 2020.
> This book provides detailed descriptions of native edibles (such as nuts, berries, and herbs) that are commonly found in the Ozarks. The author is an expert in foraging and is therefore considered to be a credible source.

Bug Identification Group – Helping Others ID Bugs. Facebook. 2020. facebook.com/groups/bug.identification
> This source is maintained by experts in insect identification and can be reliable in determining the identification of an insect.

Kuo, Michael. MushroomExpert.com. 2020. Mushroomexpert.com/laetiporus_sulphureus.html
> This website contains detailed information on mushrooms of North America. It is credible in that it is maintained by an expert in the field of mycology; it is also extensively used by new and experienced mycologists as a source for identifying and comparing various mushrooms.

Lady Bird Johnson Wildflower Center. Native Plant Database. 2020. wildflower.org/plantsmain
> This website contains information on wildflowers of North America. It is credible in that it is regularly updated by experts.

Missouri Department of Conservation. Field Guide: AZ. 2020. nature.mdc.mo.gov/discover nature/field guide/search
> This source provides basic information regarding the various plants and mushrooms found throughout Missouri. This is a highly credible source in that it is compiled and maintained by expert foragers, conservationists, and mycologists in order to provide the most up to date information possible. It is used regularly by foragers new and experienced.

Missouri Department of Natural Resources. 2020. dnr.mo.gov/
> This source contains detailed information on the various trails and parks in Missouri. Each state has its own website.

Missouri Mycological Society. 2020. momyco.org/
    This source contains extensive and detailed information regarding
    Missouri's mushrooms. It is credible in that it is regularly updated by
    expert mycologists. A quick search will reveal whether or not your state
    has a mycological society.
Mushroom Identification Page. Facebook. 2020.
    facebook.com/groups/352940311570379
    This source is run by mycological experts and can be useful in assisting
    with the identification of mushrooms.
National Audubon Society. 2020. Audubon.org/
    This source contains extensive and heavily researched information on
    North American plants, mushrooms, wildlife, and more. It is maintained
    by experts in various fields and updated regularly and is widely
    considered to be one of the most reputable and reliable guides that any
    naturalist can use regardless of field of study.
Plant Identification and Discussion. Facebook. 2020.
    facebook.com/groups/plantidentificationanddiscussion
        This source is run by experts in plant identification and care and
        can be used to obtain information about plants.
Snake Identification. Facebook. 2020. facebook.com/groups/22137638452
    This page is run by experts in snake identification. They ask that you not
    post a dead snake unless absolutely necessary.
Stone, Maxine. Missouri's Wild Mushrooms. Missouri Department of
    Conservation. 2010.
        This source contains basic yet helpful information on commonly
        found mushrooms in Missouri. Maxine Stone is an expert with
        decades of experience as a mycologist.

As you can see, many of my sources are specific to my local area. Each
state and region has its own guidebooks, websites, or Facebook groups, so I
would recommend searching for those sources as well!

WORKS CITED

Blizzard, Trent & Blizzard, Kristen. "The Modern Forager's Kit." The Modern Forager. 2020. www.modernforager.com/resources/

Dunlop, Josh. "Photography for Beginners (The Ultimate Guide in 2020). Expert Photography. 2020. expertphotography.com/abeginnersguidetophotography/

iNaturalist. Seek application. 2020. Inaturalist.org/pages/seek_app

Lady Bird Johnson Wildflower Center. Ageratina altissima. 2020. Wildflower.org/plants/result.php?id_plant=AGAL5

Missouri Department of Conservation. Field Guide: AZ. 2020. nature.mdc.mo.gov/discovernature/fieldguide/search

Missouri Department of Conservation. "Sulphur Colored Chicken of the Woods."

Missouri Department of Conservation. 2020. nature.mdc.mo.gov/discovernature/fieldguide/sulfurcoloredchickenwoods

Missouri Department of Natural Resources. 2020. dnr.mo.gov/

Ohio Perennial and Biennial Weed Guide. "White Snakeroot (Ageratina altissima)." Ohio State University. oardc.ohiostate.edu/weedguide/single_weed.php?id=91

Stone, Maxine. Missouri's Wild Mushrooms. Missouri Department of Conservation. 2010.

ABOUT THE AUTHOR

T. J. Crow is an amateur forager, writer, and author of the new best-selling guidebook, "A Forager's Guide to Appreciating Nature." As a forager who regularly wanders through the woodlands near the Lake of the Ozarks in Missouri, T. J. dreams of sharing with others the joy and wonder of the natural world. With an Associate's degree in Creative Writing and plans to pursue a Master's degree in the future, T. J. uses words with masterful precision and description to guide others into discovering and appreciating nature and all it has to offer.